THE DARK MAN

THE DARK MAN

STEPHEN KING

CEMETERY DANCE PUBLICATIONS

Baltimore

❖ **2013** ❖

Cemetery Dance Publications
132-B Industry Lane, Unit #7
Forest Hill, MD 21050
http://www.cemeterydance.com

TRADE HARDCOVER ISBN: 978-1-58767-421-1
SLIPCASED TRADE HARDCOVER ISBN: 978-1-58767-425-9

First Hardcover Edition

1 3 5 7 9 10 8 6 4 2

Printed in the United States of America

Artwork © 2013 by Glenn Chadbourne
Interior Design by Kate Freeman Design
Cover Design by Desert Isle Design

In memory of Carroll F. Terrell, scholar and friend.

I HAVE STRIDDEN

THE FUMING WAY

TRACKS AND

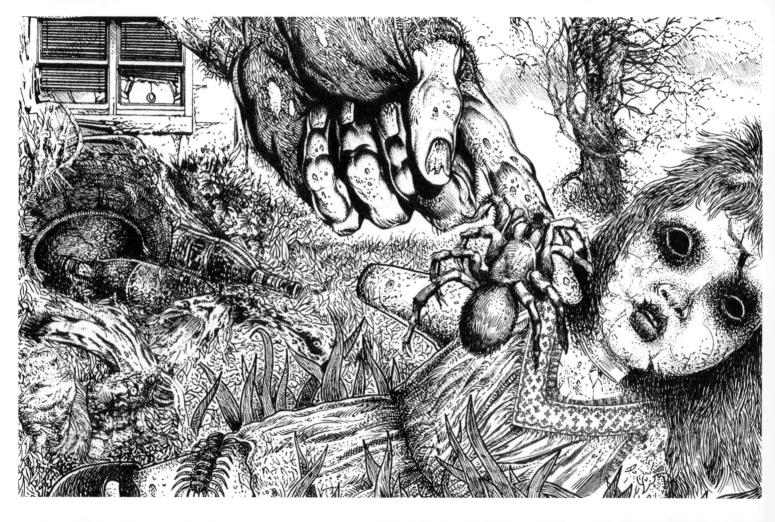

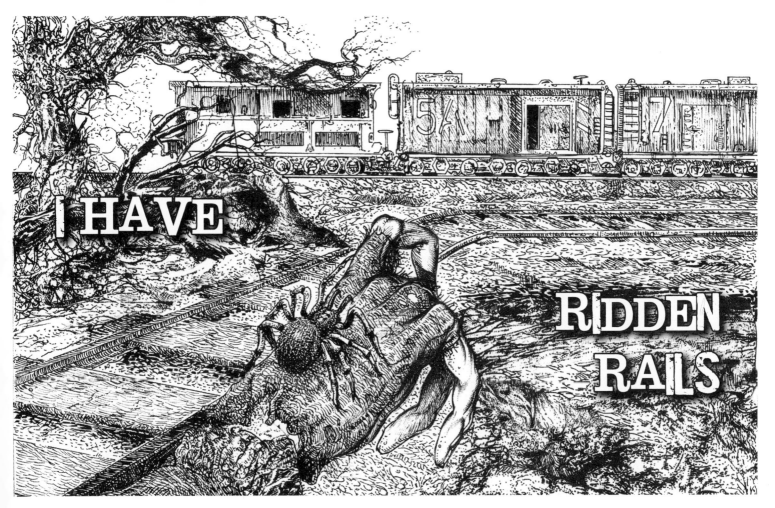

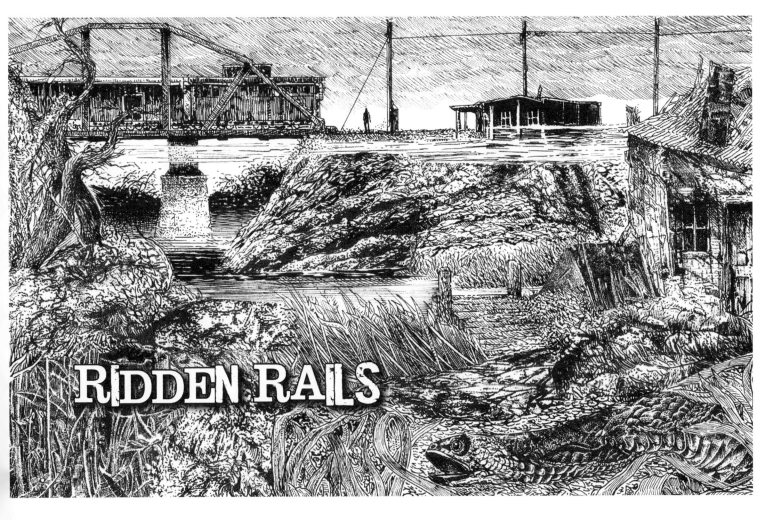

THE
SMUGGERY

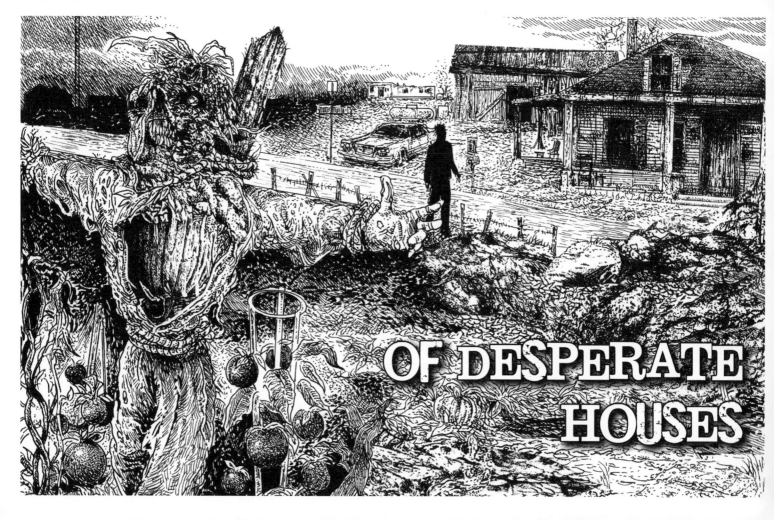

OF DESPERATE
HOUSES

WITH
COUNTERFEIT
CHIMNEYS

AND
OVER
IT ALL

A
SAVAGE
SICKLE
MOON

I HAVE SLEPT

IN GLARING SWAMPS

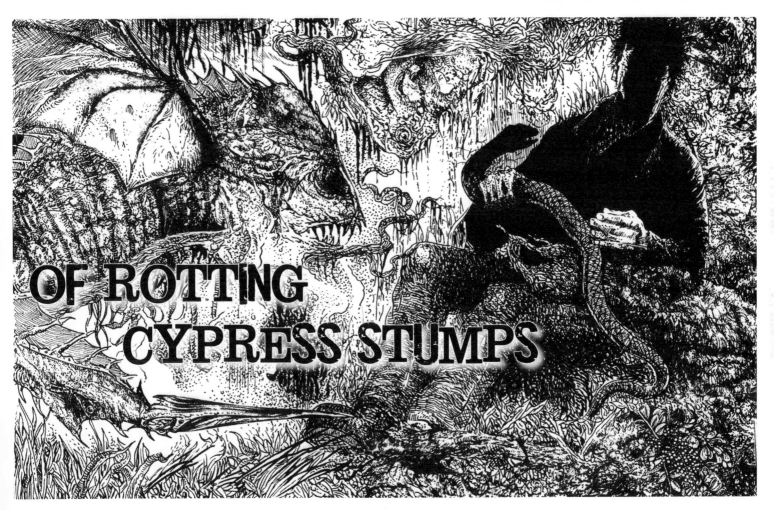

OF ROTTING CYPRESS STUMPS

WHERE WITCH FIRE

CLUNG IN SUNKEN

AND HEARD THE
SUCK OF SHADOWS

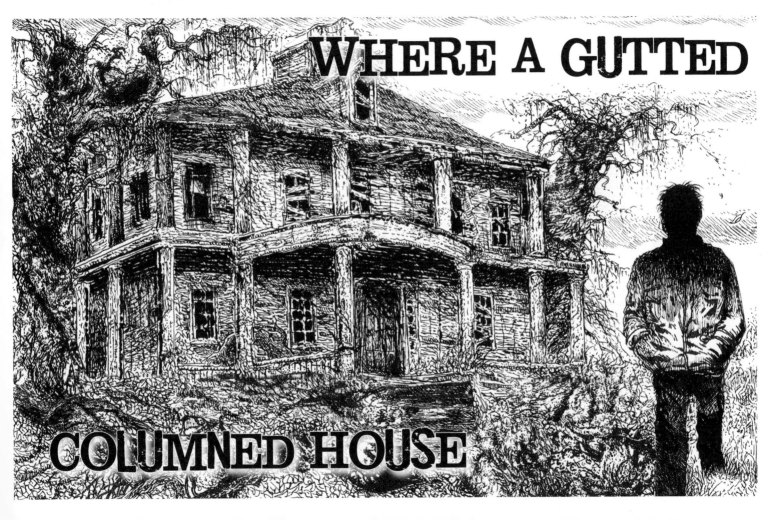

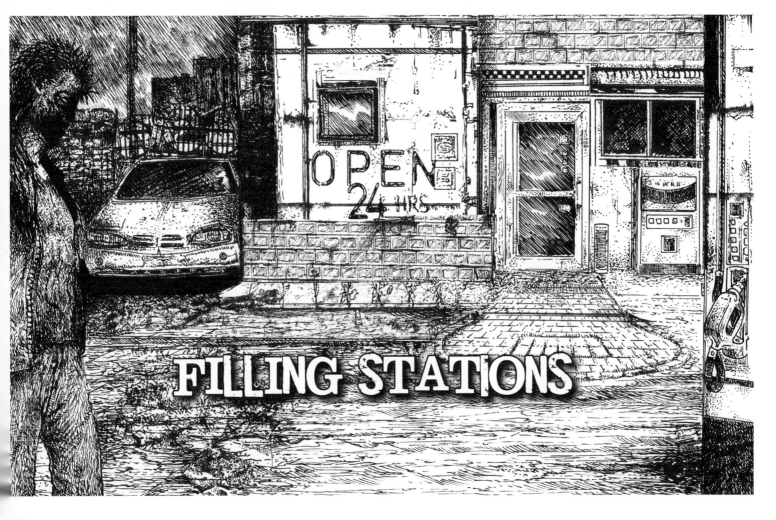

WHILE TRAFFIC IN A MAD
AND FLOWING FLAME

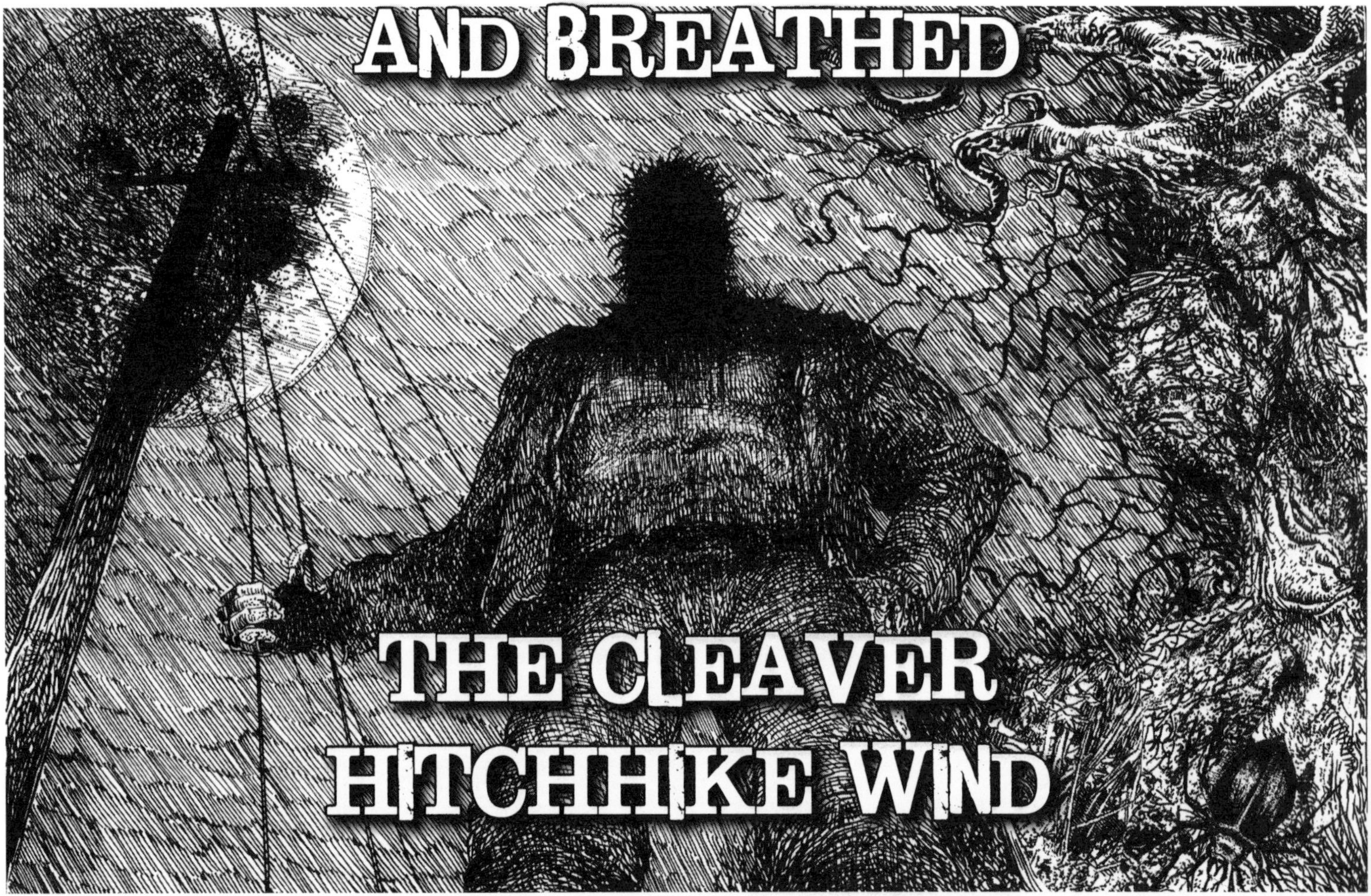
AND BREATHED
THE CLEAVER
HITCHHIKE WIND

WITHIN THE BREAKDOWN
LANE WITH THUMB LEVELED

AND SAW SHADOWED FACES MADE COMPLACENT

IN RIVEN
MONSTER
ORBITS.

FIXED WAYS:

THE DARK MAN

i have stridden the fuming way
of sun-hammered tracks and
smashed cinders;
i have ridden rails
and burned sterno in the gantry silence of hobo jungles:
i am a dark man.

i have ridden rails
and passed the smuggery
of desperate houses with counterfeit chimneys
and heard from the outside
the inside clink of cocktail ice
while closed doors broke the world—
and over it all a savage sickle moon
that bummed my eyes with bones of light.

i have slept in glaring swamps
where musk-reek rose
to mix with the sex smell of rotting cypress stumps
where witch fire clung in sunken
psycho spheres of baptism—
and heard the suck of shadows
where a gutted columned house
leeched with vines
speaks to an overhung mushroom sky.

i have fed dimes to cold machines
in all night filling stations
while traffic in a mad and flowing flame
streaked red in six lanes of darkness,
and breathed the cleaver hitchhike wind
within the breakdown lane with thumb leveled
and saw shadowed faces made complacent
with heaters behind safety glass
faces that rose like complacent moons
in riven monster orbits.

and in a sudden jugular flash
cold as the center of a sun
i forced a girl in a field of wheat
and left her sprawled with the virgin bread
a savage sacrifice
and a sign to those who creep in
fixed ways:
i am a dark man.

STEPHEN KING

Stephen King has written more than forty novels and two hundred short stories. He is the recipient of the 2003 National Book Foundation Medal for Distinguished Contribution to American Letters and he also received the O. Henry Award for his story "The Man in the Black Suit." He has released numerous special editions with Cemetery Dance Publications including *From a Buick 8*, *The Secretary of Dreams (Volume One)*, *The Secretary of Dreams (Volume Two)*, *It: The 25th Anniversary Special Limited Edition*, *Doctor Sleep*, the World's First Edition of *Blockade Billy*, and *Full Dark, No Stars*. King lives in Bangor, Maine, with his wife, novelist Tabitha King.

GLENN CHADBOURNE

Glenn Chadbourne's artwork has appeared in more than thirty books as well as dozens of magazines and comics. His trademark pen and ink drawings have accompanied the works of today's hottest genre authors. His other Stephen King Limited Editions with Cemetery Dance Publications include two volumes of *The Secretary of Dreams.* Glenn lives in Newcastle, Maine, with his wife Sheila.